CW00707068

MARY AND THE MYSTERY OF
THE INCARNATION

*An Essay on the Mother of God in the Theology
of Karl Barth*

ANDREW LOUTH

SLG Press
Convent of the Incarnation
Fairacres Oxford

© THE SISTERS OF THE LOVE OF GOD 1977

3rd Impression, reset 2002

ISBN 0 7283 0073 7
ISSN 0307-1405

Printed by Will Print, Oxford, England.

Cover picture: Icon, The Mother of God of the Sign, 13th century, Moscow.

INTRODUCTION

ON RELIGION, Discourses to the Cultured among its Despisers was the title of a little book published anonymously in 1799 by Daniel Ernst Friedrich Schleiermacher. It is the title that is significant and sets the tone for all that follows. Religion is something despised; it is an object of contempt. Sixty or so years earlier, Bishop Butler had written:

> It is come, I know not how, to be taken for granted, by many persons, that Christianity is not so much as a subject of inquiry; but that it is, now at length, discovered to be fictitious. And accordingly they treat it as if, in the present age, this were an agreed point among all people of discernment; and nothing remained but to set it up as a principal subject of mirth and ridicule ...

Butler's response was to appeal to reason; Schleiermacher's to appeal to the cultured, to the cultivated, and show them that religion was a matter of the finer feelings of mankind, something to which they—the cultured, the cultivated, especially—ought to aspire. Schleiermacher seeks to entice the elevated souls of his hearers by presenting religion as the finest accomplishment of a truly refined man: 'A religious man must be reflective, his sense must be occupied in the contemplation of himself. Being occupied with the profoundest depths, he abandons meanwhile all external things ...'

'The Church Father of the nineteenth century'—so Karl Barth styled Schleiermacher. He saw the theology of the nineteeenth century as taking its direction from Schleiermacher, and it was such theology—such liberal theology—that Barth imbibed as a student at the beginning of the twentieth century. For Schleiermacher theology was about *religion*, about man's religious consciousness; and the

1

theology of the nineteenth century on the whole accepted Schleiermacher's approach—though it was rarely as exciting as that first little book of Discourses. Such a theology, *qua* theology, was divorced from objective knowledge— *Wissenschaft*, science—which had the effect of freeing the objective, scientific study of Christian origins and history from the constraints theology might impose on it. So in such liberal theology there was, on the one hand, exacting 'independent' scholarship and, on the other, an interest in religion as the highest manifestation of the human spirit. This latter, liberal, religious theology Barth came to characterise as a theology in which speaking of God amounted to speaking of man in an awed and elevated tone.

It was this theology Barth rejected when in 1914 all his professors fell in behind the Kaiser and his declaration of war. 'It was like the twilight of the gods when I saw the reaction of [my professors] to the new situation, and discovered how religion and scholarship could be changed completely into intellectual 42cm. cannons.'[1] Barth went back to Scripture, to the Reformers, and there he discovered a God 'who is really God ... not a fifth wheel on the waggon but the wheel which drives all the rest ... not a notion, not a view, but the power of life which overcomes the powers of death ... not a feeling with which one toys, but a fact which one takes seriously.'[2]

The fruit of this was his commentary on St Paul's Epistle to the Romans, published in 1919.[3] Though printed in a small edition in Switzerland, it caused a great stir with its outright rejection of liberal theology. 'Feeling his way up the stairs of a dark church tower he unexpectedly caught hold of a bell-rope instead of the handrail, and to his horror heard the great bell ringing out above him, and audible not only to him but to others around.'[4] So Barth later described the impact of his *Romans*, recalling a childhood experience in the village church at Pratteln. The *Romans* heralded what was called dialectical theology, the theology of *Krisis*, judgement, and broke the hegemony of liberal theology, even if it did not completely destroy it. Barth, then, opened up a new era of theology—an era that turned its back on the anthropocentric and apologetic approach of liberal theology. Associated with Barth in this theology of *Krisis* were others such as Bultmann and Brunner, though they hardly formed a 'school' and quite soon were to part company altogether.

Karl Barth was born in Basle in 1886. He was brought up mainly in Berne, where his father was a professor of theology. He himself studied theology at several universities, following the German custom, both in Switzwerland and in Germany. He was ordained in the Reformed, namely Calvinist, Church and began his ministry as assistant pastor to the German-speaking congregation in Geneva. From 1911 to 1921 he was pastor in the village of Safenwil in the Aargau, between Basle and Zürich. While there he became a socialist and played an important part in the socialist movement, both in Safenwil, assisting the formation of trades unions and supporting the struggles for better conditions (for which which he became known as the 'Red Pastor of Safenwil'), and also more widely. It was during this time that his break with liberal theology occurred and he wrote his *Romans*.

The success of that book led to the offer of a chair in theology at Göttingen in 1921, and Barth went from being a village pastor to being a university professor. During the twenties and early thirties Barth held posts in Göttingen and Münster and finally in Bonn. This was a time of crisis for the West, and in Germany the menace of National Socialism was growing. Barth was outspoken in his condemnation of Hitler and Nazism and played a major part in the formation of the 'Confessing Church' which opposed the 'German Christians' who fell in with Hitler's nationalism and anti-semitism. In a letter at the time he wrote: 'Anyone who believes in Christ, who was himself a Jew, and died for Gentiles and Jews, *simply cannot* be involved in the contempt for Jews and ill-treatment of them which is now the order of the day.'[5] Barth refused to take the oath of loyalty to Hitler, required of him as a professor, and he was deprived of his chair. He eventually lost the German citizenship to which his professorship had entitled him and was expelled from Germany in 1935. Basle offered him a chair of theology, which he accepted. He still continued to play a part in the German Church struggle—though now from the outside.

During his time in Germany Barth moved beyond the dialectical theology he had sparked off with his *Romans* to his 'dogmatic theology' which found expression in his vast (over 9,000 pages), and never to be completed *Kirchliche Dogmatik*. In his dialectical theology he had confronted man with a God who smashed man's pretensions, a God before whom man was nothing, but in his dogmatic theology he found a God who was not simply Wholly Other (the great slogan of dialectical theology), but was a God who has *become* man in the Incarnation. Barth had compared his dialectical theology in *Romans* to the effect of seizing a bell-rope by mistake in a church tower. His comment on that incident explains something of the move from dialectical to dogmatic theology: 'He did it unwittingly, and he has no intention of doing it again. The effect of it is to make him continue his climb as carefully as possible.'[6] From the sheer delight in paradox and in baffling man with God's otherness in judgement and grace, Barth came to listen, to listen carefully, to the God who has become man in the Incarnation, to whom the Scriptures bear witness. A crucial step in his movement to dogmatic theology was his discovery of Anselm. In his book *Anselm: Fides Quaerens Intellectum,*[7] written 'with more loving care than any of my books', Barth analysed Anselm's theological method, especially in the *Proslogion,* with much appreciation. The *Proslogion* takes the form of a prayer; and in Anselm's search for God in prayer, pre-eminently attention to God, patient

4

waiting on God, Barth found an epitome of theological method.

His *Church Dogmatics,* begun in 1932, was his first concern for the rest of his life. He remained in Basle after the war because it seemed to him that the demands of the reconstruction in Germany into which he would have thrown himself had he returned would have hindered what he now saw as his main task. Nonetheless he was still involved in many of the political issues of the post-war era, speaking out against anti-communism and the Cold War, and against the development and build-up of nuclear weapons. In these matters he made himself unpopular with his fellow Swiss and amongst his friends in the West generally, and often enough found himself a lonely and isolated voice.

Nonetheless as a theologian he was immensely celebrated, and not only among Protestants—some of his greatest admirers and interpreters are Roman Catholics. Basle became a centre of pilgrimage; students went to sit at Barth's feet, and many distinguished theologians and churchmen made the journey there to talk with the great man. He was showered with honours: eleven honorary doctorates (in heaven he would 'certainly have to hand them all in at the cloakroom,'[8] he once remarked), and various international prizes, including the Sonning Prize which he travelled to Copenhagen to receive. ('How fortunate', he thought, 'that Kierkegaard no longer lives there and cannot object that the real prophets were usually honoured with stones and not with such prizes.'[9]) In 1962 he finally retired from his chair in Basle. The controversy over his successor, in which Barth's own choice, Helmut Gollwitzer, was rejected because of his political views, deeply hurt him and he felt that his retirement had been contrived to appear 'a kind of ignominious dismissal'.[10] He continued to live in Basle until his death, at the age of eighty-two, in the early hours of 10 December 1968.

Barth's influence in England (as opposed to Scotland) has been slight and somewhat distorted. In 1933 a translation of the commentary on Romans was published by Sir Edwyn Hoskyns. It had a considerable impact, recalling English, and especially Anglo-Catholic, theology to a serious attention to the Scriptures, and to a Gospel that does not confirm men in their better and more exalted moods, but confronts them in judgement and grace. As such its appeal was a part of the appeal of Hoskyns' own theological work. But neither Hoskyns nor his pupils were inclined to follow Barth beyond the disturbing impact of his dialectical theology. Charles Smyth in his memoir of Hoskyns, published as a preface to his *Cambridge Sermons*,[11] is very concerned to dissociate Hoskyns from the 'Barthianism' of the *Church Dogmatics*. Partly this was because little of the *Dogmatics* was available in English until the late fifties, but partly it was because Barth's move beyond dialectic to dogmatic theology was regarded as a move back into Protestant scholasticism, (back to a sort of 'black' Protestantism, or 'Protestant neo-orthodoxy') that English Catholics can safely dismiss with a slogan or two from St Thomas Aquinas. Barth's dogmatic theology, however, is rather a move forwards, a move to a closer attention to the God who embraced man's life and being in the Incarnation; or, if a move back, a truly *radical* move, that brings him more closely into touch with the roots of theology, in the Fathers and in such pre-scholastic theologians as Anselm.

In a small way, this paper seeks to show how fruitful a theological approach we can discover in Karl Barth, even in the unlikely area of Mariology. If such an expectant attention to Barth is unusual in English Catholic theology (whether Anglican or Roman), it is not so in Continental Catholicism, where Barth has long had his admirers and interpreters. One of the chief among them is the Swiss Catholic, Hans Urs von

Balthasar, and I conclude this introduction with a passage from his book on Barth:

> Barth's theology is beautiful. Not just in the external sense that Barth writes well. He writes well because he combines two things: passion and objectivity. Certainly passion for the subject matter of theology, and objectivity such as belongs to so fascinating a subject as theology. Objectivity means being absorbed in what one is studying; it means seeing it in its true proportions. And what Barth is studying is God, as He has revealed Himself to the world in Jesus Christ, to whom Scripture bears witness. Because Barth—with Calvin, against Luther—directs his attention completely away from the state of the believer to the content of his faith, because he recognises a strict theological objectivity ('the believer lives from the object of his faith'), because he distinguishes himself by that very fact from the neo-Protestantism of Schleiermacher, therefore he speaks well, therefore there is no need to fear from him mere pious edification. The subject itself edifies—builds up. But the subject itself is so exciting and demanding of the whole man, that true objectivity here involves an intensity of emotion that penetrates everything and has therefore no scope for any extraneous outlet; an emotional intensity that gives Barth's theology a shape and expression that distinguishes it from the often all too disinterested objectivity of much Catholic dogmatics.
>
> This unity of passion and objectivity is the source of the beauty of Barth's theology. Who beside him in recent centuries has been able to interpret Scripture in such a way, neither in an 'exegetical and biblicist' way, nor one-sidedly, nor with pious rhetoric, but by so completely concentrating on the Word that only this shines forth in all its fulness and splendour? And who has, without weariness, taken a deeper breath and gazed yet longer, and done so because the object of his study had developed before his eyes and begun to take expression in all its vastness? One must go back to Thomas Aquinas to find such freedom from any tension or narrowness, such peerless depth of

understanding and sheer excellence, an excellence that is not seldom touched with humour, but above all expresses Barth's decided taste for a rhythm of thought that might be characterised as *tempo giusto*. Barth knows how to convince us that for him Christianity is an altogether triumphant matter. Above all, he writes well not because he possesses a good style, but because he bears witness, completely objective witness, to his subject matter which, because it concerns God, demands the very best style, the best handwriting.[12]

Notes

[1] Quoted in Eberhard Busch, *Karl Barth: His life from letters and autobiographical texts* (Eng. trans. By John Bowden, SCM Press, 1976), p.81
[2] Busch, p.102.
[3] English trans. from the sixth German edition by Sir Edwyn Hoskyns, OUP, 1935.
[4] Busch, p.20.
[5] Busch, p.235.
[6] Quoted in Busch, p.121.
[7] English trans., SCM Press, 1960.
[8] Busch, p.489
[9] Busch, pp.467f.
[10] Busch, p.455.
[11] *Cambridge Sermons* by Sir Edwyn Hoskyns, SPCK, 1938.
[12] H.U.von Balthasar, *Karl Barth: Darstellung und Deutung seiner Theologie* (Verlag Jakob Hegner in Köln, 2nd edition, 1962), pp.35f.

'KARL BARTH AND THE PROBLEM OF MARIOLOGY.' That sounds a definite enough subject, and it is not an impossible subject, for Mariology is a *problem* for Barth. And it is a problem which exercised him from time to time throughout his whole life. Before he began the *Church Dogmatics* he had already had somewhat to say about Mary and Mariology, both in relation to Roman Catholicism on the one hand, and to Schleiermacher and his writings on Christmas on the other.[1] In the *Church Dogmatics* itself there are ten pages of small print on Mariology as well as briefer references. After he had abandoned the attempt to complete that monumental work, at the end of his long life, he wrote about the problem of Mariology in a letter to a Roman Catholic colleague.[2] In all these writings Barth is remarkably consistent. What then is the problem?

As I see it, the problem is in what *context* to put Barth's remarks. The ten pages just referred to are embedded in the section of *Church Dogmatics* called 'Das Geheimnis der Offenbarung'—'The Mystery of Revelation', or 'The Secret of Revelation'.[3] This is the section on the Incarnation. His doctrine of the Incarnation is highly orthodox and he affirms all the doctrines Catholics find associated with it: the two natures, the unity of Christ in his divine person, the Virgin Birth (or, to be more precise—though it is a precision only customary among Catholics—the Virginal Conception), and the doctrine of the *Theotokos*, of Mary as the Mother of God. Barth's treatment of these themes, as nearly always, is of great brilliance and penetration, in particular his treatment of the Virgin Birth. He does not merely assert or admit this doctrine; he gives it great prominence and probes its theological significance in a very illuminating way. So Barth presents us with a theology of virtually impeccable orthodoxy. And, more than that, with a theology which delights in this

9

orthodoxy and does not shy away from those doctrines connected with the Incarnation that involve our Lady most intimately.

However, Barth introduces his discussion of the title *Theotokos* in a rather minatory way:

> It is, as it were, a test of his correct understanding of the doctrine of the Incarnation of the Word, that an Evangelical Christian and theologian should not reject the designation of Mary as 'Mother of God' but, in spite of the burden that it is made to bear as a result of the so-called Mariology of the Roman Catholic Church, affirm and welcome it as a legitimate expression of Christological truth.[4]

There follows a brief statement of the grounds for the legitimacy and necessity of the ascription to Mary of the title 'Mother of God', which turns on the unity of the Person of Christ. The one born of Mary, the son of Mary, is none other than the Son of God; so Mary must be called the 'Mother of God', as the Council of Ephesus declared. But having said this, Barth passes to his discussion of Mariology as a characteristic Roman Catholic misuse of biblical revelation. And as he does this his remarks find another context. For Barth's theology is, in a way not at all familiar to English theologians, a *Protestant* theology. Roman Catholicism is, for him, a constant preoccupation; it represents, as it were, painted on a large canvas, clear for all to see, the many ways of misunderstanding the Gospel. A Protestant theology must protest at every turn against the consistent—and attractive— misunderstanding of the Christian Gospel by classical Catholicism. Anyone familiar with the *Church Dogmatics* will know that there are a number of themes that tend to reappear in this context. And in this *particular* context—in his discussion of Mariology—most of them do.

And so Mariology becomes for Barth part of his continuing protest against the Roman Church. This means that if we attempt to expound the pages devoted to

Mariology we are in fact led into one whole area of the *Church Dogmatics* that is not primarily concerned with Mary at all, but with the nature of the Reformation Protest—or, rather, with Barth's highly individual version of it. In this paper I shall attempt to provide Barth with a third context. I shall use what he says in the two contexts I have outlined—that of the doctrine of the Incarnation, and that of his protest against Rome—and try to show that he in fact provides a marvellous context for Mariology and yet fails to make use of it. And then I shall ask, why?

I

As we have already seen, the section of the *Church Dogmatics* that contains the discussion of Mariology is entitled 'Das Geheimnis der Offenbarung'—the secret of revelation, or the mystery of revelation. It is difficult to translate into English, and I must labour the point as it is important. *Geheimnis* can mean either secret or mystery, and here it carries overtones of both. Revelation is the unveiling or revealing of something that is hidden or secret; something is brought to view that previously was hidden. We must keep the idea that it is a secret, that in revelation we are being let into a secret. Secret *and* mystery. For what is revealed still remains a secret when it is revealed. Or rather, because the English word 'secret' will not quite stretch to that, what is revealed still remains a mystery. For we are concerned with the revelation of *God*—God who is unknowable.

When we say that God is unknowable, we do not just mean that God is infinite and incomprehensible and so beyond our mental grasp. We mean two sorts of things. First, that we can only know God if he discloses himself to us. At this level the analogy is that of personal encounter. Although at one level we find out about persons in the same way as we can find out about things—by observation, and so on—at another level such finding out is not finding out about 'persons'; I can only know someone as a person if he discloses

11

himself to me in personal communication. So when we say that God is unknowable, in part we mean that he is one who discloses himself, who makes himself known; he is not One we find out about. But now another dimension of unknowability comes to light. For when someone else discloses himself to me, I discover that he is *like* me; I recognise another being like myself. But when *God* makes himself known to me, he discloses himself as totally Other. He is not one who shares in being with me—as other persons do—but one to whom I owe the very possibility of being. So, in the language of paradox, God makes himself known as unknowable. He reveals himself as one beyond my comprehension; discloses himself as mystery. And so we speak of the mystery of revelation, the secret of revelation— *das Geheimnis der Offenbarung.*

But that is all very abstract, and God's revelation is not at all abstract. He does not disclose himself in principle; he actually discloses himself—in the history of Israel, and finally and fully in the Incarnation. So the proposition which this section of the *Dogmatics* is concerned to expand runs thus:

> The secret of God's revelation in Jesus Christ subsists in the fact that the eternal Word of God chose human being and existence, and sanctified it and took it into union with himself, so that as true God and true man, he might be the reconciling Word spoken by God to man. The sign of this mystery which is manifest in the Resurrection of Jesus Christ is the wonder of his birth: that he was conceived of the Holy Ghost, born of the Virgin Mary.[5]

For our purposes what is most important in this context is the way in which Barth treats of the Virgin Birth. For Barth, the Virgin Birth witnesses in a profound and important way to the fact that in the Incarnation we discern the mystery of revelation. In a simple and schematic way we can see what he means very easily. Jesus, *born* of a virgin, is one with us and so able to disclose himself to us; Jesus, born of a *virgin,* discloses himself to us as *other* than we are. Another way of looking at the significance of the Virgin Birth would be to say that the Virgin Birth ensures that we see the story of Jesus as the revelation of God among men, rather than a human parable about God.

All this Barth develops by speaking of the Virgin Birth as the outer wrapping of the inner significance of Jesus Christ; and it is this inner significance which is the secret—the mystery—of his Person, the mystery that makes his life, death and resurrection the revelation of God to men. The outer wrapping is the miracle of the Virgin Birth. Outer wrapping and inner meaning are not the same thing: to believe the Virgin Birth is not necessarily to believe in the mystery of Jesus' Person—it might be an unparalleled example of parthenogenesis. Similarly it is conceivable that God could have revealed himself among us without the need of the miracle of the Virgin Birth. But here Barth interpolates a warning, a warning against too ready a tendency to separate the inner and the outer. The secret of Jesus' Person is revealed in Scripture by the doctrine of the Virgin Birth, and if we sit light to the latter it is all too likely we shall let slip the former; if we deny the Virgin Birth, or treat it as a matter of indifference, it is all too likely that the mystery of the Person of Jesus will seem to us explicable, comprehensible—perhaps as a parable of God's love for men, instead of the incomprehensible mystery of God's presence among men. So when Barth discusses Brunner's treatment of the Virgin Birth in his book *The Mediator*,[6] where Brunner sees the miracle of the Virgin Birth as an example of 'biological inquisitiveness' about the miracle of Incarnation, Barth, as he puts it, makes his own the groan uttered by Nicolas Berdyaev:

I have read [writes Berdyaev] Brunner's book with great interest, because I feel in him sharp and exhilarating thought and religious pathos. When, however, I came to the place where Brunner confesses that he does not believe in the birth of Jesus Christ of a virgin, or at least that it is a matter of indifference, I became sad at heart, and the matter became boring. And it seemed to me that everything cancelled out and all the rest was pointless.[7]

Barth in fact, as is well known, puts the Virgin Birth on a par with the empty tomb. The Virgin Birth is not the Incarnation, nor is the empty tomb the Resurrection. But dare we separate the inner meaning from the outer expression in either of these cases?

I think I have said enough to indicate that for Barth the Virgin Birth is not simply something implied in two or three passages in the New Testament; it is not simply one of the facts accompanying the narratives of the birth of Jesus, like the shepherds or the wise men, say, but is the outer historical wrapping of the whole significance of that birth, and so rightly enshrined in the Catholic Creeds. As we pass from believing the Virgin Birth to believing in the Virgin Birth—that is, grasping not just the fact but its significance—we come to belief in the Incarnation of the Son of God; we come to see disclosed in the life, death and resurrection of Jesus the mystery, or secret, of revelation. The Virgin Birth is not simply admitted as a fact, but invested with deep, theological significance; and this significance is tied up with our apprehension of the mystery of God's self-revelation. But for Barth this leads to no reflection about our Lady, to no Mariology. Why not?

II

To begin to answer that question let us turn back to his ten pages on Mariology in the section where, as I mentioned earlier, he discusses the title 'Mother of God'. This title, he says, is really a Christological title, for all that it is ascribed to Mary. When the Council of Ephesus said that of Mary it did so in order to say something about Christ. However, Mariology is interested in Mary for her own sake. Barth stresses that for at least the first five centuries of the Church's

14

existence, and really for much longer, there is no *independent* interest in Mary. Even the idea of Mary's continuing virginity is found in a context of Christological and not Mariological interest. The parallel Eve/Mary is, in origin, but an aspect of the parallel Adam/Christ and is again Christological—though Barth notes that the development of this parallel can easily become arbitrary or wilful. Barth gives two reasons for rejecting Mariology: first, that against Scripture and the early Church it represents an innovation which is—again—arbitrary or wilful; and second, that this innovation involves a falsifying of Christian truth. These are fairly sober words compared with what follows. He quotes an antiphon from the Third Nocturn of the Common of our Lady, *Cunctas haereses sola interemisti in universo mundo* ('You alone have destroyed all heresies in the whole world'), and goes on: 'If that is a fair expression of Roman Catholic systematics, then it means that the doctrine of Mary is no more and no less than the central critical dogma of the Roman Catholic Church, the dogma from which all its different positions can be seen to develop and with which it stands or falls ...' and so on.[8]

Barth is now in full sail. How, he asks, is this to be explained? How is it that the doctrine of Mary is so decisive for Catholic theology? It is not—and here Barth completely dissociates himself from a common Protestant prejudice—that Catholics ascribe to Mary a divine or quasi-divine status. In fact quite the opposite. 'The Mother of God is purely a creature'—so Thomas Aquinas, quotes Barth. Mary is no pagan goddess but a creature; indeed it is precisely *as* a creature that she is exalted.

> In spite of her infinite dignity, in spite of her matchless privileges, in spite of—no, just because of—her co-operation in redemption, she is no Goddess, she does not belong to the realm of being of the Trinitarian God but, on the contrary, quite over against that, she belongs wholly and completely to the creaturely sphere, and indeed to the earthly-human-creaturely sphere.[9]

But if Mary is simply a creature, how is it that the doctrine of Mary has developed? In answer to this Barth proposes an antithesis between the physical fact of her divine motherhood ('the biblical doctrine', as he calls it), and Catholic doctrine based on her willing assent to the divine invitation. He sees that it is not in virtue of her divine motherhood that Mary possesses the importance she has for Catholic Mariology, but in virtue of her acceptance of God's will for her; and this Barth calls, in language which from him is loaded, her 'bridal relationship' to God:[10]

> The crucial fact, in virtue of which she acquires her dignity and her privileges and on the basis of which she is capable of that co-operation, is not purely her physical state of being Mother of God as such, but the accompanying bridal relationship to God expressed in her: 'Behold the handmaid of the Lord. Be it unto me according to thy word.'[11]

It is here that Mariology becomes a problem for Barth and where the picture he has built up turns into a caricature and robs him of any further chance of understanding the doctrine of Mary. He agrees that Mariology does not make a goddess of Mary, that she is seen precisely as a creature. And he agrees that the mere physical fact of her involvement in the mystery of redemption is not what provides the springboard for Mariology. But what does provide that springboard, he rightly sees, is her *willing co-operation* in the mystery. And for Barth this at once suggests the idea of some capacity on the part of the creature to establish a point of contact with God— and such a capacity he utterly rejects. And so from this point on Barth is no longer thinking of Mary's humble obedience to God but is irresistibly drawn back to the familiar phrases and categories of his polemic with Rome.

In the introduction to the first volume of the *Church Dogmatics* Barth makes his famous attack on the doctrine of the analogy of being *(analogia entis)*, the idea that God and the creatures share together in existence. 'I hold', he wrote, 'the *analogia entis* to be the invention of Anti-Christ, and think that because of that one cannot become a Catholic. Therefore I hold that any other grounds for not becoming a Catholic are to be regarded as short-sighted and lacking in seriousness.'[12] The doctrine of the analogy of being sums up for Barth a whole category of his fundamental Protestantism, his fundamental rejection of Catholicism. He held—wrongly in fact—that the doctrine of the analogy of being in Catholic theology implied that there is some common ground between God and creatures, a common ground due to their both sharing existence, or being. Once any such common ground is admitted, then God no longer confronts the creature in revelation as wholly Other; the secret of revelation is dissolved, the creature can approach God on the basis of this similarity.

It is all this that Barth is evoking when he quotes Aquinas' dictum 'the Mother of God is purely a creature' and then goes on to talk of Mary's co-operation with God, Mary's bridal relationship to God. Why should not Mary be on a level of co-operation—even equality—with God if in virtue of the analogy of being all creatures have a fundamental likeness to God? In its Mariology Catholicism manifests that attachment to the doctrine of the analogy of being 'because of which one cannot become a Catholic'.

Barth presents a superb picture of Mariology; but he does so only in order to plunge in the knife. He is right, but only that he may be the more unfair. But in being unfair to Catholic Mariology he is, above all, unfair to himself. His implacable Protestantism makes him clothe his presentation of Mariology in terminology drawn from the most fundamental category of his rejection of Roman Catholicism—viz. the doctrine of the analogy of being— which means that he only sees what Mariology is about in order to reject it. And having rejected it, it remains a door firmly closed. Thus when he comes to discuss the Virgin

Birth, as I have outlined above, there is no chance of his seeing how what he is saying might lead to an important way of understanding the true significance of Mariology.

III

The Virgin Birth points to the mystery or secret of revelation; it points to God's unveiling of himself by his veiling of himself in a human form. Mary, the virgin, in her assent to the divine invitation, becomes the Mother of God; she becomes the veil that conceals God in order to reveal him. She brings forth for us the secret of revelation; she makes possible for us our access to that secret. But we cannot treat all this as a mere physical fact, as a mere external historical wrapping of the inner truth of God's disclosure of himself to man. Barth has already warned us about separating the inner and the outer, but we might wonder whether he is not really guilty of that himself in some measure. For what of Mary's part in all this? If God's revelation is what we know it to be—the revelation of God's love—then it cannot be satisfactory to think of Mary in merely physical terms, as if she were nothing more than the vehicle for making possible the incarnation of God's love. She must be taken up into this mystery as a person—loved by God and responding in love. But what we find in Barth is an opposition of notions that makes it impossible for him to begin to entertain any such reflection. Physical divine motherhood on the one hand; bridal relationship, evoking images of a pagan sacral marriage, between Mary and God on the other. The opposition is too sharp. Mary *is* physically the Mother of God; but her involvement in the mystery of revelation cannot be purely physical if this is the mystery of the revelation of God's *love*. And bridal relationship to God would be marvellous if Barth would let himself think of the traditional interpretation of the Song of Songs,[13] if he could allow himself to be sensitive to the typology of Luke's infancy narratives where Mary appears as the Daughter of Zion, as Israel consummating the covenant in her *Ecce ancilla Domini*—for then we would be a long way from the associations of a pagan sacral marriage.

Indeed Scripture itself will not let us so separate the outer historical role our Lady plays and her inner involvement in the mystery of redemption. Nowhere in all his discussion of the mystery of revelation does Barth make any reference to Luke 2:19: 'But Mary kept all these things and pondered them in her heart', which is repeated in verse 51 and, so to speak, underlined. Inner and outer cannot be separated: what Mary bears in her womb she also ponders in her heart. But by ignoring the inner meaning of Mary's part in this mystery, Barth does here separate inner and outer, and in so doing he, in effect, foreshortens his understanding of God's mysteriousness. He stresses, as we have seen, the mysteriousness of the revelation of the Unknowable God. But he seems to miss the inner significance of such mysteriousness. He uses the doctrine of God's unknowability to cut away any human pretensions in our knowledge of God. But it goes deeper than that, for the unknowability of God really points to the endless richness of God, a source of endless wonder and contemplation. 'And the Word was made flesh and dwelt among us, and we *beheld* his glory, the glory as of the only-begotten of the Father, full of grace and truth ... . No man hath seen God at any time; the only-begotten Son, which is in the bosom of the Father, he hath declared him.' (John 1:14,18.)

The mystery of the revelation of the unknowable God in the Incarnation is apprehended in the *beholding* of the glory seen in the Incarnate Word: and Mary is the type of that contemplative wonder and adoration. It is a short step from this to the doctrine of Mary's immaculate conception or what is, if not exactly the same thing, an expression of the same insight, her all-holiness, Μαρία Παναγία. For this is concerned with the subjective conditions of such a contemplative receptivity to God that, in her *fiat* and her becoming the Mother of God, there should be no gap between the personal and the physical—for any 'gap' would mean that God was dealing with Mary as less than a person. But if the end is love, the means must be love too. Similarly, it is a short step to the doctrine of the Assumption, which is concerned with the consequences of such contemplative receptivity or, to put it another way, with the eschatological dimension of contemplation. Clearly if such contemplation were conceived of in a platonic vein—immaterial contemplation of timeless reality—no such implication would hold. But if contemplation is an anticipation of the final revelation of God's glory then such a consequence becomes difficult to escape. Indeed, one could only really escape it if one saw contemplation as accidental to the Christian life rather than as its core, but John 1:14 does not give us that option. For 'the Word was made flesh and dwelt among us, and we beheld his glory, the glory as of the only-begotten of the Father, full of grace and truth.'

IV

'We know instances of Christians', says Lossky, 'who, while recognising for purely Christological reasons the divine maternity of the Virgin, abstain from all special devotion to the Mother of God, desiring to know no other mediator between God and man than the God-man, Jesus Christ.'[14] Barth is clearly one of those Christians, and as such he is representative of classical Protestantism. Liberal Protestantism usually does not even recognise the divine maternity of the Virgin, for the Christological reasons have ceased to be cogent enough, the Christology having become diluted—though, as Barth several times points out, that does not prevent a romantic devotion to our Lady as perfect woman, or perfect mother. One refrains from comment on that. But can we say anything about *why* classical Protestantism gets thus far and no further? Here I do not think Barth is a good example—or not a typical one, anyway. For Barth opens up a way that leads further. Let us look, then, for a moment at one I would regard here as a *typical* representative of classical Protestantism, and that is Austin Farrer.

Austin Farrer treats Mariology *ex professo* in an article, 'Mary, Scripture and Tradition'[15] and what he shows, in a way both brilliant and ingenious, is that the doctrines about Mary *clearly* implied in Scripture—by which he principally means the Virgin Birth—can be held, but no others. What I find odd about Farrer is the tremendous emphasis on *clarity*. In absolute contrast to Barth, Farrer presents us with ingenious arguments for holding that certain truths are facts; but having got these facts I am not at all sure what one is expected to do with them. This is the trouble with the classical Protestant attitude to our Lady. The doctrines simply remain propositions. They have no context, no *real* meaning; they do not lead us into prayer. But doctrines that do not lead us into prayer are not at the deepest level theological at all, for theology is about our relationship to God.

Of course, Farrer *does* want to say something about Mary. But the doctrines do not seem to me to be deployed by him in their true Christological context; rather they are facts about one of the saints, to wit, our Lady. The doctrine of the Virgin Birth secures the idea that Mary has a peculiar relationship to Jesus, and Farrer seems to suggest (if this is not too unfair a way of putting it) that this will be of topographical significance in heaven. Even less than with Barth is Mary seen as actually being part of the mystery of redemption. I find in Farrer an ultimate rationalism at this point. He can assert various propositions about our Lady; but if he admits the possibility of any devotion to her—and I would imagine he does—it is because she is one of the saints, and devotion *is* paid to the saints. This is a long way from either Catholic or

21

Orthodox Mariology, which never becomes independent of the mystery of the Incarnation.

Which never becomes independent of the mystery of the Incarnation. Barth fails to understand Mariology not because it is heretical but precisely because it is not. For Barth Mariology is independent *(selbständig)* and that is the root of the trouble. And in a curious way it seems that Farrer develops just such an independent Mariology, for the dogmas about our Lady that Farrer can accept are not developed in their Christological significance so much as used to secure Mary a special position among the saints. But, as I see it, Mariology is about none of these things.

In Catholic and Orthodox Mariology the dogmas of our Lady are derived out of, and retain their significance in the context of, Christology. They disclose Mary's role in the mystery of redemption. Mary is not independent; she does not stand by herself. She is the Mother of God, deriving her meaning and significance from our Lord; and she is herself, a woman, one of us. As Mother of God she discloses to us the mystery of revelation; and as we seek to contemplate that mystery we find ourselves kneeling by her side.

Barth's problem is that he is so afraid of Mary's going into orbit, so to speak, in the heavens as an independent being, that he cannot recognise her real independence, as one of God's creatures, as one of us. His treatment of the Incarnation is almost entirely masterly, bringing out the ultimate mysteriousness of God's disclosure of himself in the Incarnation, and the part played by the Virgin Birth in this disclosure. But he dare not see Mary in this context, for he is afraid that if we see her here at all we shall see her between ourselves and God, as *mediatrix* and *co-redemptrix*. And in this Barth, it seems to me, falls victim to fundamental flaws in Protestantism and, ironically enough, to two such flaws which his whole theological effort was concerned to oppose, those of rationalism and individualism.

So, he seems to think, if in my response to the mystery of redemption, I discern something of our Lady, then I must be looking at her and not at God, I must be putting her between God and myself. But not so: Mary stands beside me as one who helps me to contemplate the wonder of God disclosed in the Incarnation. I do not just apprehend what is before my eyes—that is the error of rationalism which ignores everything not articulated in concepts. I apprehend the whole situation in which I am. And in the mystery of revelation Mary is there: for without her that mystery would not have been disclosed. Barth's ultimate rationalism prevents him from seeing this. His individualism shows itself as we realise how Barth is interpreting the fact that, in his revelation of himself, God lays hold of me at the most intimate depths of my being. That is certainly true, but it does not follow that I am conscious of a purely individual relationship to God. On the contrary, the more deeply I apprehend God in myself, the more deeply do I apprehend others in God—and the first among those others is Mary. For it is in Mary's *Ecce ancilla Domini* that the possibility of fallen man's being gathered up into the unity of Christ becomes an actuality.

Barth in his development of the mystery of the Incarnation takes us to the beginning of a way that leads to a profound and deeply significant Mariology. He could not and would not tread this way himself in his earthly life,[16] but we can be grateful for what he has opened up to us. Here we find an interpretation of the Virgin Birth not just as an event more or less adequately attested in Scripture, but as disclosing to us the mystery of the revelation of the unknowable God. Mary, the Mother of God, is an integral part of that mystery. As we seek to contemplate the glory of the Word made flesh, we kneel beside her whose willing assent made it possible, and who herself 'kept all these things and pondered them in her heart'.

NOTES

[1] See, e.g., *Theology and Church* (SCM Press, 1962), pp.136 ff., 307ff.

[2] *Ad limina apostolorum* (Evangelischer Verlag, 1967), pp.61ff.

[3] *Die Kirkliche Dogmatik* I, 2, (Evangelischer Verlag, 1939), pp.153-160. (English translation—hereafter abbreviated ET—published, all volumes, by T. & T. Clark and Scribner, New York, 1956 onwards, pp.139-146.) A smaller type-face is used (what I have referred to as 'small type') for the passages where Barth discusses other theologians, gives detailed exegesis of Scripture, and defends his own interpretation as expounded in the main text. The discussion of Mariology forms such a section.

[4] Ibid. pp.151f. (ET p.138.)

[5] Ibid. p.134. (ET p.122.)

[6] ET by Lutterworth Press, 1934, pp.322ff., 361-2.

[7] Quoted in *Kirchliche Dogmatik* I, 2, p.201. (ET p.184.)

[8] Ibid. p.157 (ET p.143). It ought perhaps to be mentioned that in the letter referred to in note 2 Barth no longer holds the idea that the Marian dogmas are *that* central to Roman Catholic theology.

[9] Ibid.

[10] The phrase 'bridal relationship to God' is taken, more or less literally, from the *Handbuch der katholischen Dogmatik*, vol. 3, by the late nineteenth century Roman Catholic theologian, M.J.Scheeben, whom Barth was to describe as 'certainly the greatest figure which the Roman Catholic Church has recently produced in the German sphere'. (Busch—see note 1 in the notes to the Introduction—p.413.) In his *Handbuch* Scheeben puts the idea of Mary as the bride of God into a biblical context which Barth practically ignores. In isolation the phrase cannot but contain for Barth suggestions of a pagan sacral marriage, which he naturally rejects.

[11] *Kirchliche Dogmatik* I, 2, pp.157f. (ET p.144.)

[12] *Kirchliche Dogmatik* I, 1, pp.viiif. (ET p.xiii.)

[13] Barth has, indeed, some very interesting things to say about the Song of Songs later on in the *Dogmatics*, but he never brings any of this to bear on Mary's relationship to God. (On the Song of Songs see *KD* III, 1, pp.358-361 (ET pp.313-316), III, 2, pp.354ff. (ET pp.293ff.).)

[14] *In the Image and Likeness of God* (Mowbrays, 1975), p.196.

[15] In *Interpretation and Belief* (SPCK, 1976), pp.101-125.

[16] In 1966—two years before his death—Barth was received 'literally with open arms' by Pope Paul VI. Barth later related in a letter that during their hour-long talk, 'we also touched on the difficult point of Mariology: the Pope had heard that I would prefer Joseph, the foster-father of Jesus, as the primal image of the nature and function of the Church, rather than the *ancilla Domini* who was later elevated to the rank of queen of heaven. He assured me that he would pray that in my advanced age I should be given a deeper insight in this matter.' Quoted in Busch, p.484.

ALSO PUBLISHED BY SLG PRESS

The Victory of the Cross
Dumitru Staniloae

The Psalms: Prayer Book of the Bible
Dietrich Bonhoeffer

George Herbert, Priest and Poet
Kenneth Mason

Pilgrimage of the Heart
Benedicta Ward

Theology and Spirituality
Andrew Louth

A full list of publications is obtainable from
SLG Press Convent of the Incarnation Fairacres Oxford OX4 1TB.